The Poetry of Laurence Binyon

Volume VI - Penthesilea

Robert Laurence Binyon, CH, was born on August 10th, 1869 in Lancaster in Lancashire, England to Quaker parents, Frederick Binyon and Mary Dockray.

He studied at St Paul's School, London before enrolling at Trinity College, Oxford, to read classics.

Binyon's first published work was Persephone in 1890. As a poet, his output was not prodigious and, in the main, the volumes he did publish were slim. But his reputation was of the highest order. When the Poet Laureate, Alfred Austin, died in 1913, Binyon was considered alongside Thomas Hardy and Rudyard Kipling for the post which was given to Robert Bridges.

Binyon played a pivotal role in helping to establish the modernist School of poetry and introduced imagist poets such as Ezra Pound, Richard Aldington and H.D. (Hilda Doolittle) to East Asian visual art and literature. Most of his career was spent at The British Museum where he produced many books particularly centering on the art of the Far East.

Moved and shaken by the onset of the World War I and its military tactics of young men slaughtered to hold or gain a few yards of shell-shocked mud Binyon wrote his seminal poem *For the Fallen*. It became an instant classic, turning moments of great loss into a National and human tribute.

After the war, he returned to the British Museum and wrote numerous books on art; especially on William Blake, Persian and Japanese art.

In 1931, his two volume Collected Poems appeared and in 1933, he retired from the British Museum.

Between 1933 and 1943, Binyon published his acclaimed translation of Dante's *Divine Comedy* in an English version of terza rima.

During the Second World War Binyon wrote another poetic masterpiece *'The Burning of the Leaves'*, about the London Blitz.

Robert Laurence Binyon died in Dunedin Nursing Home, Bath Road, Reading, on March 10th, 1943 after undergoing an operation.

Index of Contents

Penthesilea, queen among the Amazons inhabiting the Euxine coast of Phrygia, having unwittingly killed her own sister, and the fame of Hector's death by Achilles being brought over the mountains to the ears of her people, leads her chosen Amazons to Troy; she means to challenge the victorious Achilles, and in battle throw away her life for atonement of her sister's blood. Priam receives her, at first with doubt and incredulity of the prowess of a woman, then, persuaded by her speech, welcomes with some rekindlings of hope. At night she is visited by Andromache, who had supposed her a goddess come to avenge her husband's slaying. Their mutual anger, relenting, and farewell. On the morrow the Greeks, unready for battle, are set on by Trojans and Amazons and driven back to their ships, till Achilles, at first scorning to fight in such war, assails the Trojans in the centre; their confused rout and slaughter on the banks of Simois; Penthesilea's vain quest of Achilles through the disordered battle, till at last he returns from pursuit; their meeting and single combat: the queen dies by his hand, but in dying fills the soul of her conqueror with love.

PENTHESILEA

I.— THE COMING OF THE AMAZONS

Dark in the noonday, dark as solemn pines,
A circle of dark towers above the plain,
Troy sat bereaved; her desolation seemed
To have drawn slowly down in sultry drops
The sky of gathered and contracted cloud,
Hung silent, close as is a cavern roof,
That deep in heavy forests, lost from day,
Echoes the groans of a hurt lioness
For her slain cubs; she fills her den with groans,
Stretching her hoarse throat to the flinty floor;
And with like lamentable echo, barred
Within the great gates, dirge of women swelled
Along the dark-door'd streets that lately shone
With Hector's splendour as he strode to war,
Wailing for Hector fallen; upon towers
Unchampioned men grasped idle spears and groaned.
But in the heart of Troy dead silence dwelt.
There to a temple, throned on a green mound,
Andromache was stolen; there she bowed
Her widowed forehead, pressed upon the strength
Of a square pillar; not a sob, nor sigh
Passed from her, but immovably inclined
She waited yet expected nought; that hour
Of grief was on her, when the exhausted flood
Of passion ebbs, and the still shaken heart

Hungers for staunching silence: then the touch
Of patient cold stone is desired like bliss.
So mourned Andromache, unmoved to know
If earth that lacked her Hector, still endured,
Absorbed into the vastness of a grief
Only by its own majesty consoled.
Crouched at her feet the child Astyanax
Played on the slabbed floor with the creviced dust,
Or followed with soft parted lips and eyes
Bemused, the foiled flight of a swallow's wings
That, strayed within, sighed swiftly up and down
The temple gloom; there was no other stir
In that hushed place of stone, while the slow day
Declining moved the sullen cope of heaven
With westering breezes; under brooding cloud
Light newly trembled; looking up, the boy
Saw wide sheen in the portico that laid
Long shadows from the pillars. It was then
A faint and clear sound in the distance rose,
He knew not what, but wondered, as full soon
Troy seemed to stir and waken; it drew nigh
Up the steep street, a noise of horses' hooves
Numerous and gallant with the ring of arms.
He rose up, and on soft feet tripping stole
To the porch-pillars, looked forth, and returned
Bright-eyed, back to his mother; thrice he twitched
Her robe, ere she perceived; then slow she turned
Her face down on him; bending so, she changed
As a sky changes when the unmuffled moon
Steals tender over April's vanished rain;
And love, older than sorrow, filled her eyes
A mother's, not a widow's now. With awe
In his quick voice the boy cried, 'Mother, come!
The Goddesses ride up to fight for us.'
Andromache smiled on him; though she heard,
Scarce sought to understand; and yet it seemed
Those soft lips brought an answer from afar
As oracle or dream to her sad soul,
That long had waited; she too heard that sound,
And as impetuous freshet in the spring
Breaks on a stagnant stream, the bright blood-warm
Extravagance of hope shot like a pain
Through her dulled body; then her heart recoiled
On doubt and trembled, though the noise now near,
Mingled with cries and swarm of running feet,
Drew her steps on; beside her pressed the boy
Exchanging wonder with his mother's eyes,
Till on one knee she dropt, and holding him

In jealous-clasping arms close to her breast
Looked to the door; now thronging heads appeared
Beneath the temple steps; and they beheld
Framed in the wide porch men and women pass,
And over them, proceeding proud and fair,
Like goddesses indeed, a wondrous troop
That glorified the sunlight as they rode
With easy hips bestriding their tall steeds,
Whose necks shone as they turned this way and that,
Bold riders on bold horses; light mail-coats
They wore upon loose tunics, over which
Where to the throat the stormy bosom swelled
A virgin shoulder gleamed; for now the fire
Of evening, struck back from the temple wall,
Burned ardent hues upon them, moving past
Untamable as their own steeds that moved
With them, and beautiful with ice-bright eyes,
Glancing around them strange, and tossing hair;
Flashed upon bronze bits of the horses, flamed
Along smooth brown wood of their javelin-shafts
To the bright points, and radiantly repelled
From hilt and helm, glowed changing upon shields
Like moons in August, like a hundred moons
Of moving brilliance; scarves of coral red
Blown from the baldric, trembled like the fire
In eyes that kindled the beholder's soul
To presage of what fury these fierce queens
Should madden with, when they were loosed to dance
The dance of battle, matched with men or gods,
Wild as the white brooks when they leap and shout
In tumult, tossing down the wintry hills.
So filled with wonder the thronged faces saw
Those terrible and lovely huntresses,
Mid whom one rode yet queenlier than the rest,
With steadfast eyes superb; a spirit crowned
She seemed, the votaress of some far desire;
She turned not like the others, but rode on
Like one that follows a star fixt in heaven,
Fixt as her thought is; whom beholding now
Mourning Andromache with closer arms
Entwined her boy; her heart was full, it pressed
Against her side, invoking that strange hope
That here was the avenger of her loss,
A sword brought from afar; she leaned at gaze,
Following that form, impassioned to divine
What purpose charmed her from the world of men.
When lo! the street was empty, all had passed.
She rose and with uncertain motion stood,

Swayed like a slender poplar when the south
Tremulously bows it, over her dear child,
Who clung upon her fingers looking up
Wide-eyed with joy: together they went forth.
Already fast as over an ebb shore
The fresh tide rolls up with a rising wind
Invading dry ledge and deserted pool,
And ere the seaward rocks be over-stormed,
Streams gliding with a soft stir far inland,
So fast through Troy the stir of rumour ran
To every hushed house; every chieftain heard
Indoors and sent forth messengers to see.
Even to Priam's palace it was borne.
Then there was hurrying through the empty courts,
And women drawing water at the wells
Set down their pitchers; boys ran out; it seemed
As if a city of sleepers sprang to life,
A thousand beating hearts. Priam alone
Heard not at all, for none was with him now,
But solitary in that pillared hall
Where he had feasted with his glorious sons
In days of old, sat patient, mournful, rapt,
His chilly limbs warmed by a cloak's long fold,
In such December solitude of mind
As when the last leaf glides to frozen earth
And all the boughs are bare: the days to come
Were darkness, and the past days like a sea
Of roaring waters; vacant unto each
He mused upon the evening gold that fell
Aslant a pillar's roundness, holding up
One hand against the fire that burned beside.
He heard not, saw not, though without the sound
Of opened gates and murmuring hubbub fast
Increasing on the distance, gathered in
As to the silent centre where he sat
Alone in gloom, nor noted how behind
Came stealing steps; Cassandra first, the shunned
Of all the happy, who yet disbelieved
The fate of her foreseeing; others next
Of Priam's house, mid whom the heavenly eyes
Of Helen, like a mirror to the doom
Coming on beauty till the end of time,
Shone in their sadness; beautiful she leaned
On fair flushed Paris of the golden head.
They as they entered stood expectantly
Pausing, although the King still sat entranced,
Clouded in sorrow's deep and distant reign;
Until Cassandra touched him on the arm

And his eyes woke; a sad, astonished gaze
He lifted; in that moment the far door
Was opened: lo, upon the threshold gleamed
The splendour of an armed Amazon
Coming towards him; her eyes sought his own:
Slowly, and yet without a pause she came;
And those that saw her deeply breathed; she moved
As if a clearness from within inspired
Her motion, challenging their inmost thoughts.
Simplicity ennobled all her ways;
The heart leapt at the turning of her head;
But in her eyes a soul, deep as the night
Filled by the beauty of assembling stars,
Night on lone mountains, could shine out sword-keen
As now, though touched for Priam's woe she gazed,
While, slowly stirred, he lifted up to her
His brow, and it was kingly: now he seemed,
Though seated, in his stature to resume
Old majesty; for princes of the East
Had sued to him, and Asia sought his word
To hearken to its wisdom. Some few steps
The Amazon approached; at last she spoke.
'Art thou the royal Priam?' 'What seek'st thou,'
He answered, 'of an old unhappy man?'
'I seek,' her voice rose ardently, 'to bear
My arms against Achilles in thy cause,
To hazard in the venture all I may
For Troy and thee, King. This is my quest.'
Proudly she spoke; but he, as old men will,
Because he wondered, was displeased, nor knew
How to rub clear the dimmed sense of his grief,
And pausing half incredulous replied,
'What hast thou said? Abuse not these old ears.
Thou know'st that I have suffered — who art thou?
A woman! Art a woman, and would lift
Thy hand against Achilles? Never hand
Of man prevailed against him yet, and thou
A woman made to bear and suckle babes,' —
'A woman,' she broke in, 'but not as those
Who spin at home and blench to see a sword.
Penthesilea am I called, and am
An Amazon, and Amazons I rule.
They call me queen; but I like them was reared
To suffer and to dare; my body bathed
In cold Thermodon can outrace his speed;
And I have slain the lion in his lair,
Yea, and have fought with men and have prevailed.'

Admiring murmur followed on her words,
From those that hearkened with hope-kindled eyes.
Priam said only 'Hector fell.' That word,
Slow-spoken, not to her, but in the dark
Of his own grieving mind, dropt like a stone
Down a well's echoing silence. There was pause.
Just in that moment stole Andromache
Over the threshold; then her heart drank wine,
For she beheld Penthesilea there,
Moved but not shaken, like a Goddess stand
Of all regarded, while her spirit seemed
To swell within her on some secret wave
Of strength, and lifting up her queenly head
She spoke like music through the darkening hall.
'One certain night I stood upon our hills
Before the dawn was come, and I beheld
All the stars over me from south to north
And east to west, each in his place, as they
Had shone before I was or thou, King.
And as I looked, one fell: far down the sky
It shot in fire to nothing. Who might think
One of heaven's splendours, fixed in heaven, could fall?
O Priam, even Achilles, even he,
This far-renowned one, shall be overthrown
For all his glory and his might, perhaps
By hand unguessed, and thou behold him fall,
It may be by another, or by me.'

Yet Priam would not be persuaded, nay,
Clinging to his old lamenting thoughts, he cried:
'There was none brave as Hector, and he fell,
Hector is fallen; snap all swords in two,
Break all your bows asunder, as my heart
Is broken: it were better. What avails?
What wouldst thou, Queen?' Yet even as he spoke,
Gazing upon the noble Amazon
The strong bonds of his grief were loosed awhile.
There seemed a courage in those shapely arms,
In that clear brow, which to refuse might be
Unpardoned of the gods: her clarion words
Rang through him still; and as a traveller tired
Vacantly resting at the long day's end
Under the hollow of a stream's high bank
Hears rushing over him the beat of wings
And sees a wild swan snowy-throated take
His effortless great flight in the sun's beams,
So Priam saw her! bound afar to lands
Of morning, like the beauty of those wide wings,

Free, where he might not follow, left alone
In the fast-falling night; but oh, not so,
Not bound afar, but at his feet, with eyes
Of proud petition, of a sweet command,
Penthesilea like a vision stayed
And her voice breathed one silver summons, Hope!

A hush took all who listened, then they stirred.
Only Cassandra, crouching by the King,
Hid her dark face; the others, nearer drawn,
Looked upon Priam, and his soul was moved,
But not as they; his gaze now at the full
Answered the clear magnanimous regard
Of her that spoke with pity, as he replied,
'What sad word hast thou uttered! Oh, thy lips
Are young that shape it, ere they understand.
Look on me that was once called happy, Queen!
What knowest thou of ill? I have borne more
Than my young fears, stretched by some childish wrong,
Imagined that the whole world could contain,
Or this frail flesh that pens us in our place
Find possible to bear. I have been taught.
None was so blest in sons, and none so curst.
And now I know not if the Gods be kind
Or if 'tis the last cruelty they use,
That having heaped such evil on our heads
They lend us power to bear it. O speak not!
For I can teach thee how men learn to bear;
'Tis not with fortitude of hope increased,
'Tis with dulled sense that thickens on the soul
And all its longings pined in frost that cramps
The quivering heart up, till it feel no more.
I am so knitted in harsh fortuned root
As tottering towers, in bitter fibre bound
That props what it has killed. Yet I endure.
Why wilt thou trouble me? For thy young face
Pricks with its courage like reviving blood
In a numbed arm. I was at peace, O Queen.'

He ended, and the glorious Amazon,
Moved even to tears, stept toward him and knelt down
And touched his knees, entreating: ' Let me learn,
Even though the price be of such utmost pain
As thou hast tasted: I would prove my heart,
That is prepared for all things: let me go!
I am not all so ignorant of grief.
Grant me this boon, that I may fight for thee.'
Priam heard marvelling; bending o'er her, soft

He laid his old hands on her youthful hair,
Answering: 'Is thy heart so fixed indeed?
Ah, child, is not life sweet? Turn again home
In honour, for so surely as I live
And as Troy stands, thou shalt have honour here.
The hazard is too much. I, that have ploughed
This heavy and hard furrow into Time
Cannot turn back, but thou canst. Wilt thou not?
None shall reproach thee. O too much ere now,
Too much, too dear blood in my cause is spilt.
And thou art dear and shalt be always dear
And thy name named with blessing in my house.'
Penthesilea lifted up her head.
She looked on him and smiled. 'I thank thee, King.
And thou art wise and I am foolish, yet
Though Heaven in thunder did forbid me this
My heart is fixed.' Then Priam sighed, she rose,
And he made answer: 'Be it as thou wilt
And I will say some good thing of the Gods
Since they have raised a woman's heart so high.
Bring torches, for the Queen shall feast with us
This night, and on the morrow if she will
Go with our battle forth. Bid Troy prepare.'
So Priam ordered, and the chiefs obeyed.
Through all the city ran the word for war,
And swords refurbished gleamed in kindled eyes
At hope of help unlooked for: Troy was glad,
And all the Amazons that night held feast
Among the captains in the torch-lit halls
Of Priam's royal house. At his right hand,
Admired of all, Penthesilea sat,
Still in her bright mail, though unhelmeted;
For when she had bathed, they brought her women's robes
But she refused; for in her heart she thought,
I shall be deemed but as a woman is
And they will put no faith in me for deeds.

How strange the hush was of the glimmering room
In a high tower apart, when after feast
And song were ended, and all gone to rest,
Penthesilea sat beside the bed
Whereon her coat of mail, now laid aside,
Shone keenly crumpled into glittering folds
Next the smooth texture of a coverlet
Embroidered in dim Indian town with shapes
Of golden lions thronged by suns and stars;
A Tyrian rug was soft to her bare feet
When kneeling by her side Harmothoe

Had loosed their sandal-thongs, and bathed them both
In warm clear water from a brazen bowl;
Who now was gone; and the Queen, left alone,
Stood up, and let the loose white robe fall free,
Holding her strong hands clasped behind her head,
While through their fingers streamed the heavy hair:
She sighed, — a fierce sigh panted from her breast,
Like some imprisoned leopard's, ill at ease
In those rich walls that held her from the air,
And with faint subtlety of old perfume
Wrought on her sense remembrance, as through dream,
Of what dead women fair in idle hours
Had here adorned them, pacing with soft feet
The coloured stones inlaid upon the floor,
Parting these curtains with their silver rings
To gaze upon a mirror, kneeling down
Beside the ebon coffer, to search out
Within its depths of robe laid over robe
Some beaten armlet of Assyrian gold,
Jade-brooch or branches of rose coral brought
From far bays of Arabian Astabel;
Foreign and fair devices; dream on dream,
In the low lamp-flame's wavering, oppressed
The panting free heart of the Amazon.
Thus as she leaned with heavy-lidded eyes
Backward, and into grandeur slow rebelled
The strong mould of her breast beneath the throat,
Andromache stole in to her; she stood
With wondering gaze fixt faltering in the door
A moment, then, hope trembling at her lips,
While the warm blood rushed up her cheek, she ran
Swift to the other's knees, and falling cried,
'O Goddess, help! Ah, surely thou art come
From heaven to avenge me, for the gods in heaven
Loved Hector well; thou hast a woman's shape
But mov'st not like a woman, no, nor look'st.
O certify my heart, my wounded heart,
Fill me, for I am empty; turn again
The water of life into this stony bed
Where my days used to run. I am alone.
Reveal thyself, if to none else, to me.'

Penthesilea with stern looks amazed
With both hands on her shoulders put her off,
Saying, 'Who art thou? What wild thought is thine?
Rise up, kneel not, embrace not so my knees,
My arms are stronger, nay, look up, behold,'
Then with a milder voice continuing,

'I am no goddess, feel, my heart beats quick;
I am not calm as the gods are in heaven.
This flesh is mortal, strike and it will bleed,
Has bled ere now; and feels thy wound and throbbed
To hear thy supplication, and to see
How like a bird thou droppedst to my feet!'

Andromache sank backward on her knees,
Wide-eyed with fearful doubt, then slowly rose
And stood apart, cold now as if despair
Had closed about her sudden as dark night;
Like thunder-drops her words fell desolate:
'O my great hope, how easy was thy lure,
How sweet and now how bitter to my taste!
The folly of my fond heart bites my heart.
The gods are loth to be revealed when they
Take among men disguises: but oh no,
Thou art a woman, thy face speaks the truth.
And yet, yet, if a woman, whence and why
Comest thou, what madness pricks thee so to dare
What scarce a God might compass, when my own
Great Hector whom none else could vanquish fell? '
But now the Amazon regarding her
More earnestly, spoke heedless of her cry,
'I saw thee in the hall where Priam was.
Art thou not Priam's daughter?' 'Hector's wife,'
Answered the other. 'Then I know thy name,
Andromache men call thee; and I know
Thy wound: sit by me, be my friend to-night,
Tell me of this Achilles, I would know
What manner of a man is he who sounds
In the world's ear so terrible. Is he
Fair-haired, as I have heard, or swarthy-cheeked
Like those men I have matched my strength against,
The Gargareans? Do his inches tower
Much over mine? How goes he into fight?
On horseback, as we Amazons, or afoot?
Or standing in a chariot hurls his spear?
Tell me of all these things, that I may know
And be aware and in the battle take
What vantage may be mine among the Greeks
The better to avenge thee, if fate will.'

Andromache said no word for a space,
Facing her with dulled eyes and mind confused;
Then to her lips a word outleapt her thought
Fledged with a bitter meaning: she exclaimed,
'Thou lovest him!' The queen laughed, a scornful laugh,

'O woman, have you none but woman's thoughts?
Because you are weak and have such clinging arms, —
I felt them soft and trembling round my knees —
Deem you such weakness rules an Amazon?
What is this love you are so quick to find
The key of all you cannot understand?
To tremble and to wait on a man's mood
And seek I know not what bliss in his arms
That fondle you a plaything, far from all
The thoughts that make him strong! Such thoughts I have,
Such will to tame and conquer, such delight
In battle, such resolve never to yield
My soul to any other's servitude.
Love, love! Think you I have been wont to bathe
My body in snow-brooks to temper it
True as a sword-blade, slept on forest leaves,
Raced the wild colts to break them, chased the deer,
The lion even, seen the red blood spirt
Of men into whose murderous eyes I looked
And did not quail, think you that such as I
Have hung my life's joy on another's smile,
Pining with fancies such as in close walls
You women fill slow days with feeding on,
Who lie upon soft couches and dream dreams? '

She ended with an anger-burning eye
Standing dilated in her beauteous scorn
Over against Andromache, who shook
Her head, distrustfully insisting still,
'Yet, yet thou lovest him.' 'Suddenly a fire
Swept o'er her and impatiently she cried,
'When thou hast borne a man-child, speak of love!
Thou knowest not, thou, though in thine ignorant heart
The blind beginnings of that selfsame power
Compel thee where it wills, where thou wouldst not.
Thou hast not loved, thou hast not known a man,
Yet a man's glory, a man's imagined form
Has drawn thee from thy mountains even here,
To meet him face to face. Ask thy heart why!
Hate, hope, fear, longing, 'tis all one; 'tis love
Betwixt a man and woman. Ah, didst think,
Penthesilea, to escape? But now
Necessity has overtaken thee.
Achilles masters and o'ertops thy mind
Who wouldst be wooed not with soft words but spears.
And thou must seek him. To thy wooing go!
But oh, thou goest into a fell embrace,
For he will clutch thee as a hawk a hare,

And thy bride-bed shall be the bloody ground.'

With that harsh word she would have turned to go
But stayed upon the threshold; for the voice
Of Penthesilea called her, changing now
To a deep cry, not angered nor in scorn
But grievous, as though suddenly her heart
Imperiously swelled beyond its bounds
And loosed its secret storm and sweetness out,
The proud voice breaking into truth and pain.
'No, no! not so, thou shalt not leave me so,
Thou dost not know me; far away thy words
Fly over me, they hurt me not at all.
Yet, didst thou know my heart — I am not wise
In love, thou say'st, yet I am wise in grief.
'Twas not Achilles drew me; it was grief
That drove me hither, grief brims up my heart
And blinded me to thy grief: sit by me,
Andromache, and hear me: nay thou must.
I had a sister, whom indeed I loved,
For we were twinned in thought and act and soul,
My bedfellow and playmate; oft have we
To one another brought a timely arm
Faint in the heat of battle or of chase.
But oh, it was this arm, that should have first
Withered on the shoulder, this right arm that sped
The bolt that slew her, my Hippolyta!
She had outstript me on the woody hills
Hunting a hind that fled us; I saw not;
But where the boughs were stirring in the brake
I drew my bow, the arrow leapt, I ran,
Parted the hazels, and beheld her there
Lying beyond, the arrow in her side,
Where still I see her on soaked yellow ferns
Under a thorn, trailed with black bryony,
So near a pool, the fingers of her hand
Could touch the trembling harebells on its brink.
She bled within, — there was no blood at all
To soil her body that still seemed to live —
Nor gave a cry, but with one hand she beat
On the wet ground a little, then was still.
But when I took her by the hand, it hung
Cold in my grasp, though close I cherished it,
And kissed her cheek, her mouth a hundred times,
Calling upon her name, Hippolyta:
Calling the dead that heard not. — I have seen
When Euxine on a sudden rises black
With storm, a sail that sought our haven swept

Out into darkness, from the cliffs have watched
How it flew onward fearfully, far out
Blind under sheets of tempest and was lost.
From that hour I drove like that driving ship
Borne on, I recked not whither, over wastes
Of time that have no harbour and no peace.
I fled, and yet I feared being thought to flee.
Therefore did I imagine to my soul
Some dear atonement that should make my name
Burn on the lips of men; set up my mark
And that pursued, till the usurping hope
Of glory with a glozing tongue sometimes
Flattered my dark thoughts to forget: but oh,
It is myself that am pursued, the hounds
Of memory are upon me, — Break this off.
Too much is spoken. Yet my heart is eased.
Forget this weakness, tell not to another
Penthesilea's sorrow, for from now
She puts it from her, she is strong again.
Nay, from my childhood up 'twas in my soul
The dearest hope to do a thing of fame.
To-morrow I will slay thy husband's slayer,
Or gladly, if the fates refuse, will die.'

While she was speaking, sad Andromache
Changed in her countenance, her soft bosom swelled
And her eyes brightening were soon dimmed with tears.
At last she broke forth: 'O unhappy Queen,
Pardon!' But ere another word could pass
Her lips, there was a babbling cry without,
Soft feet came running to the door, and there
Parting the heavy curtain, stood the child
Astyanax, who ran to her and called,
'O Mother, I have found thee. Come to bed;
I woke and could not find thee, and was afraid.'
The old nurse following at his heels began
To chide him, but Andromache embraced
Her boy and kissed him; he looked wondering up
Now at the Amazon and spoke in awe,
'It is the Goddess, mother '; when again
She hugged him close, and gentle came her voice,
'Penthesilea, pardon! I have erred,
My hope was blind and my despair was blind.
I dreamed of Gods come down to succour me.
Lo, here is my avenger! ' and she held
The boy before her, while the warrior queen
Admiring his bold limbs and fearless gaze
That wandered to the splendour of the mail

Lying on the bed, uplifted with a smile
The sword beside it, saying, 'Wilt thou fight
With such a sword when thou art grown a man?'
Whereat he gravely answered to her face,
'Yea, I am Hector's son.' Andromache
Drawing him towards her, with warm kisses, spoke
'I keep thy father's sword for thee; but now
Thou must to bed and sleep. Sleep also thou,
Penthesilea; and to-morrow morn
Eat with me ere thou go, and thou shalt have
All such as Hector's heart delighted in
When he went forth to battle. Fare thee well.

Penthesilea was alone. She turned;
Lo, in the corner the moon's wandered beam
Lay gentle, like the soul of solitude.
She drew a curtain; over earth the night
Rose naked; and she looked with longing eyes
Past the low plain, where Simois wound his stream
To choke in marsh mist and the creeping ooze,
Up to the mountain tops, and far beyond
Saw in her memory clear a certain glen
Where snows among the pale cloud gleamed above
Crag-pines, but from the spongy mosses sprang
Tall ash and chestnut, plundered by the gusts
Of autumn to let fall gold leaves adrift
Upon the young Thermodon, that between
Grey boulders, dancing in his frolic race
Over the abrupt edge of a gloomy gulf,
Leapt and was lost; but lost in splendour! so
Should her life be ennobled in its end,
Lifting her heart she prayed, and in her mind
Knew how, removed from all that others use
And have their joy in, she must fix her course
One way, since exiles in the world of men
Heroic hearts are unto the end alone.

II.— THE BATTLE

Waters of Asia, westward-beating waves
Of estuaries, and mountain- warded straits,
Whose solitary beaches long had lost
The ashen glimmer of that sinking moon,
Listened in darkness to their own lone sound
Moving about the shores of sleep, when first
A faint light stole, and hills in the east emerged,

A faint wind soon, born upon ocean, blew;
The cold stars faded; high on forest slopes
The goatherd woke in his thatched hut and shook
His cloak about him, striding forth, and saw
Pale over the round world of shadow tower
The silently awakened presences
Of Rhodope and Ida, dawning peaks
Far opposite, that slowly flushed, till all
The hill-thronged vales streamed out in sudden gold,
He saw the young sun ripple into fire
Propontis, and the bright seas run like wine
Into the dim west where aerial snows
Of Athos hovered o'er a hundred isles;
Nearer, Troy towers stood gleaming; in the plain
The river smoked with mist, and cranes in flocks
Rose through the sun-soaked vapour toward the sea
Beyond the trench and trench-encircled huts
And black-beaked Danaan ships upon the strand.

There in their huts and tents the Danaans woke,
And streamed abroad in the keen morning air,
But armed not yet; their camp made holiday,
With shields hung up, with heads unhelmeted.
Greek challenged Greek to hurling of the quoit,
To wrestle and race; not a sole trumpet rang,
For Troy since Hector's slaying kept her gates
Fast-barred, nor sent her files forth to the war.
So now the battle-weary Greeks prepared
Their meal beside the trenches, eased at heart,
When single scouts came running from the plain:
'Arm, arm!' they cried, 'for Troy will fight to-day,
The Amazons are come to succour them.'
Then sportful laughter leapt from mouth to mouth
Among the gay-eyed youth, mocking to hear,
And one to another shot a mirthful word.
'The hawk is dead, the twittering swallows come
To harry us! We will go garlanded
To. battle and will hale these women home.'

So as for sport they armed; but ere the word
Had run through half the camp, Thersites rose,
Filled with his dwarfish malice that rejoiced
In quarrels without causes between friends,
Pleased with the comedy of angry wits
When wisest men show weakest; he arose
Glancing from side to side in evil glee,
And went along the sea-beach till he came
Where lay Achilles and his Myrmidons

Who pitched apart, a separate host; he went
Alone, for all despised him though they feared
His tongue, and coming to Achilles' tent
Called to him with a gibing pomp of speech.
'Hail, son of Thetis, slayer of thousands, hail!
Hear what fresh tidings echoes through our camp!
Thy fame is flown into the Asian lands,
And how thou didst, a goddess helping thee,
Hew Hector down, provokes the envious world
To emulate thy glory. Lo, to-day
Troy's latest hope, there comes to challenge thee
A woman.' Then Achilles laughed aloud,
But he continued: ' Nay, it is a queen,
Penthesilea, Queen of the Amazons,
Brings her wild squadrons to this faint-heart Troy,
A queen of fame, with courage like a man's
And more than woman's beauty. Agamemnon
Already in his gloating thought adorns
His palace with this all-outshining gem
Captive to him. O Eagle of the Greeks
Doth not the quarry please thee? ' But again
Achilles laughed: 'Come, yet another day
I shall have peace and leisure from the fight.
I wore a woman's robes once, feigned their ways
In Scyros, and I know them, quick to fire
Upon imagination of a deed
That blazes through them like a strand of flax
Left light as ashes, fluttering, when the hour strikes
For doing what a man's heart leaps to do.
On such Achilles draws not. Get thee gone,
Thersites, let the Greeks fight if they will
With these mad women: but my heart is stirred
To be alone and think upon the dead
This day. Thy wry face puts me out of tune.
Begone, thou crookedness, ere thou be driven!'
So trudging back with ill smiles on his mouth
Thersites went, well pleased to bear bad news.

Achilles stood at his tent-door; the sea
Before him smiled; but heavy thoughts like rain
Clouded his darkening spirit, as his eyes
Looked homeward toward the far Thessalian coast
Where he was nurtured in fresh upland glens
Of Pelion, and his father even now
Kept his old age, watching uncomforted;
But most the thought of dear Patroclus' dust
Drew his soul down to sorrow; pacing slow
The shore he came to where the mound was heaped

On those beloved ashes; there he bade
Fetch wine, and poured libation to the dead.
There came a runner hasting from the camp,
Who cried: 'Achilles, arm! The battle joins;
And half our host, yet unprepared, recoils
Before the onset of those Amazons
Whose horses rush upon them, and they cry,
Where is Achilles? Arm, and bring us aid.
'Tis Agamemnon sends thee this command.'
But Peleus' son looked frowning and replied,
'Go tell the King I heed not his command
Nor any man's; to-day my sword is sheathed.'
With that he turned him to his grief; the peal
Of distant horn and crying of many cries,
All the harsh drone of battle muttering swelled
Beyond the trench and rows of stranded ships
Half-sunk in sand, that with their rampart shut
The beach into its calm of little waves
Falling and hushing; but to Achilles' ear
That roar was vain and hateful; and he drew
His cloak over his head, and cried with groans,
'O to what end, what end? Must our souls beat
Their high-attempered force out, and keen edge
Blunt in a senseless turmoil, but to make
A pageant for the Gods? O friend, I lose
How much more than thyself in losing thee!
Have I appeased thy ghost, and given thee sleep
By my so great revenge? Yet am not I
Appeased. Because in courage and in strength
The Gods have made me excellent beyond
All other sons of men, this is my woe
That none can match me, easy comes the crown
Of glory, and I would toss it from my hand
Into these careless waters, could I find
Some stay and dear abode such as I found
In those thoughts that together, O my friend,
We held, and well-companioned, ever looked
On through all days with never sated eyes.
But now the splendour and the spur is gone.
I hunger after thine untimeliness
For which my tears were shed. O that these Gods
Who smile on their calm seats in happy heaven
Could be provoked to wrath and themselves come
Against me armed; then were there scope and marge
For this full fire to burn in, that consumes
My soul in puny angers at the pomp
Of Agamemnon's puffed authority.
But me they mean for some inglorious doom,

And even now, plotting my shame, have sent
A woman to defy me! ' Thus he cried
Pacing in angry grief the calm sea-sand,
While still the noise of war, rolled nearer, charged
The air with jarring clamour; noon was passed,
And the sky strewn with slow clouds idly moved;
But ever louder at the trench it rose.

At last a second runner from the camp
Came, and Achilles knew him as he ran;
It was a youth from white Iolcos town
Of Peleus' kin; he sobbed forth breathless words.
'Come to the trench, Achilles, come and see!
Not women are these Amazons but wolves!
Like Maenads, maddened beyond strength of men,
They rage and with amazement bear us down.'
So both went forth to the great dyke and looked
Over the trench; then in Achilles' heart
Grief straightway slumbered, and the cruel sting
Of battle stirred in him: as one who sees
A wild bright bay of angry ocean storm
With thunderous upleaping, surge on surge,
Black rampart rocks, filling the brilliant air
With sound and splendour, and joy charms his eyes,
So now rejoiced Achilles; not less fierce
In onset than those waters snowy maned,
The Amazons on their wild horses rode
Storming upon the stubborn infantry,
And by them, thrice-inspirited, with shouts
Of vengeance, the victorious ranks of Troy.
Achilles looked far o'er the fray and laughed:
'See how the sullen Ajax like a bear
Stung by a bee-swarm, puzzles how to strike:
But you shall see how these same Maenads fly
When that I leap upon them. Say, I come.'
Glad the youth turned, and ran back to the Greeks,
And through them flew the word 'Achilles comes.'

Penthesilea through the press all day
Had sought for Hector's slayer, and sought in vain,
Though many a captain on her path in arms
So tall, so splendid stood, that hope had sprung
Not twice or thrice alone that this was he
She should defy; the rest she scorned, yet some
Essayed her prowess and came wounded off
Or fell beneath her, and so trampled, died.
Lo, as a potter strikes with eager hands
Shapes of soft moulded clay, fired with the thought

To make a thing more noble, so she smote
Those meaner challengers, crushed idly down
If haply from the wreck and tumult might
Spring the desired Achilles; her bright axe
Shone over shouts and groans and maddened more
The tempest of those headlong Amazons
Who rushed black-maned upon spurred horses, where
The spears bristled the thickest. They outmatched
The fury of impetuous Diomed,
Who even now where fierce Antandra struck
Hardly avoided, catching at her rein,
And was borne backward raging in his beard
With half his helm-plumes shorn away; with her
Derione and Thermodossa, red
With rapture of the sword, Antibrote,
Hippodamia and Brontissa drave
Like screaming gusts of whirlwind when the air
Fills with torn boughs of cracking oaks, and pines
Shiver to ground uprooted; thrust on thrust
Met shrieks, where desperately tugging hands
Clutching a spear were tost up suddenly
As it stabbed home; strange-echoing female cries
Exulted; in the van Harmothoe
Called, as her axe-blows rang about her path
Hard as the white hail when it strips the vines
And their bruised clusters; the gay Danaan youth,
Spoiled of their sweet imagined sport, laughed now
But as the mad in whom no mirth is, driven
Before the Amazons in pale amaze
And terror of their beauty and their strength,
While crest on crest the Phrygians followed on.
But most all marvelled, friend and foe, to see
Clear where the foremost onset hurled and clanged,
Penthesilea like a star in storm
That through the black rents of a burying cloud
Rides unimperilled; for none stayed her, not
Diomed, nor Ajax; yet her quest despaired;
Achilles came not; something failed the hour,
And ere he came 'twas lost: there at the trench
In baffled frenzy the wild warring queens
Perceived it in their hearts, and raged the more,
Wanting the one goal's glory that should force
Their last strength onward; by so much as they
Began to faint, by so much more the foe
Rousing his stubborn manhood, clenched his ranks
And bore them backward. Then Achilles came.
He leapt upon the dyke, bright as a brand
Breaking to sudden fire; they saw him shine,

They heard his great voice clear above the roar,
And half the battle swerved along the plain
Toward Simois. Far upon the city wall
Andromache was gazing; now she pressed
Her hands upon her bounding heart in fear;
She saw her own host in the centre break
Before Achilles and roll back; in vain
Penthesilea on the seaward wing
Maintained the onset; half her Amazons
Caught in the frayed edge of the flight, were turned,
Were flying; nay, it seemed that earth and heaven
Joined in that altered combat and pursuit,
For in the west the sun charged out of clouds
And shot his rays forth over shadowy isles
Set in the fiery seas, and flashed behind
The Argives and their crested coming on,
Dazzling the ranks of Troy, that broken now
Reeled from the middle outward, here and there
Stemmed by a chieftain's cry; with hot-blood cheek
The youthful Troilus was storming, shamed,
And shouted: 'Rally at the river bank!'
But now among the fleers thudding hooves,
The maddened steeds of single Amazons,
Headlong and helpless, thrice confounded them,
In whom the terror of Achilles stung
Sharp as a cruel rowel in the flanks
Of those scared horses; uncontrollably
Crushed, wrestling, groaning, trodden, all were hurled
Together wild as from a foundered ship
A hundred men, flung forth, one moment strive
Huddled in the hollow of one tremendous wave,
The next upon its crest toss up to crash
Down upon rocks they agonise to shun:
So desperate in a huge blind tide of flight
Phrygian and Amazon together reeled.
All in a moment they had reached the stream.
A grove of oaks stood on the hither side,
Where Troilus made rally some stout hearts
Staying the rout. Woe then to him that fled,
When in his back the pouncing arrow plunged
And straight was bloody to the feathers! woe
To him that fled, there was no help for him!
Ingloriously he fell, or pressed by shields
Of comrades from behind was beaten down,
Or on the crumbling bank was crushed by hooves
That broke the bones in many a breathing breast
Of strong men, trampled like tall mallow stalks
At the stream's edge, broken like leafy boughs

That cracked and splintered in the whirling stroke
Of swords; and many falling in the stream
Meshed by long weeds were strangled in the ooze.
Black-haired Antandra there, forced with the rout,
Strove ever like a raging lioness
To turn on her pursuers: on the bank
She stayed her horse, and some Thessalian youth,
Stung by her beauty, caught her by the belt
And dragged her from the saddle; she, so spent,
Let fall the axe from her dead-weary arms,
But with sobbed breath caught him so desperately
That both together in a blind embrace
Fell plunging in the shallows, rolled among
Marsh-marigolds; she thrust upon his face
Under the water, laughed and strove to rise,
When even then a javelin bit her breast
And clove her through; so died Antandra; so
Fell many another; pity there was none,
For cruel is the anger of men shamed
When they avenge their shame; and that fierce hour
Made many a widow on far hill-town wall
That golden evening dandling with fond smile
A son already fatherless; and still
Achilles'' murderous and resistless hands
Were stayed not. So by Simois the red flight
Streamed swift and fearful as a fever-dream.

But meanwhile upon either wing the war
Swung doubtful, nay, the Greeks were overmatched,
Wanting their champion, drawn with all his men
So far dispersed, though now shrill trumpets rang
Recalling them, for on the seaward side
Penthesilea pressing hardly, she
With the fierce remnant of her Amazons
And grey Antenor, passionately smote
As in a kind of anguish; like a net
Trapping a lion's limbs the battle closed
Round her deep-thwarted spirit: Sthenelus
Assailed her, striding huge among the rest;
And riding at him, as she struck, the axe
Crashed broken on his helm, she wrenched the spear
From his stunned arm, when on the other side
Leapt Ornytus against her, and she swerved
To dart the spear-point through him, crying out,
'O that thou wert Achilles!' All at once
Clear from the distant battle's farther edge
Sounded upon a sudden several horns,
Harsh-blown bull's horns; Antenor knew the note

Of signal, and he called across the spears,
'Penthesilea, hark, upon the left
The son of Aphrodite holds the day.
Between us all the foe is locked and hemmed,
And hot Achilles has pursued too far.
Press, 'tis Troy's hour!' and even as he spoke
The Greeks relaxed; but now, flushed from the rout,
Those same pursuers singly and in troops
Mixed in the battle, all confused, and swung
A score of ways with half- arrested clash
And crossing tides of onset; streaming loose
In separate combats, or bewildered pause
Where all was doubt. Penthesilea burned
Amid the scattered mellay; surely now
From Simois through the dust and disarray
She spied a great crest and a blazing spear
Returning, and Harmothoe cried out,
'Penthesilea!' with so keen a cry
That her heart leapt; she knew Achilles came.

All knew, the spent arms and the shouting heads
Were stayed and turned; they halted man by man
As knowing the hour was other than their own,
Awaiting in a thrilled expectancy,
As a drawn bowstring ere the arrow fly,
That strange encounter, not alone the shock
Of chosen champions, but a storm of worlds
Where the deep blood-tides, man and woman, met.
Penthesilea kindled, her soul soared
Above the beating of her heart, alone
Answering that high peril, that made pale
The boldest round her, all their fluttered hope
Afraid, as with a deep imperious cry
And striding pace, through moil of crimsoned arms
Dinted and shattered shields, Achilles came
Shining from head to heel; a demigod
Whom smouldering anger dyed in fire, whose limbs
For swiftness and for strength unmatchable
Seemed but the prison of a spirit that, freed
As a flame leaps in beauty to and fro,
Splendid in indignation should have towered
Against the lords of heaven; a spirit wronged,
That for oblivion of its sore heart-strings
Had robed itself so red in slaughterous deeds
And as in scorn feasted on dying cries,
Hot like a reveller seeking to forget;
But as a reveller comes out into dawn
Shooting bright beams up to the fading stars,

So was it with Achilles when he found
The royal Amazon; in ardour she
Leaned on her reined horse forward, all her soul
Ingathered at a breath, ready to launch
And dare, as those together-leaping looks
Like stone and steel flashed! To the fingers tense,
She poised in one uplifted hand her spear
Against him over challenging proud eyes,
That quailed not where the eyes of kings had quailed.

'Turn again home! Thou canst not fight with men,
And least with me, whom no man overcomes,'
Scornfully with a mighty voice he cried,
'Madwoman, turn, or here thou spill's t thy soul!'
Clear rang her voice back, < Put me to the proof!
Have I not sought thee, Achilles, all this day,
And having found thee, shall I let thee go? '
With that she hurled, and the spear bounded forth
Straight at Achilles' face, but lifting up
His shield, he caught it on the golden boss
That shivered it to pieces: his own spear
Flew on the instant, the shock marred his aim,
And not the queen he smote, but smote her horse
Deep in the shoulder, with sharp shriek he reared
And staggering fell; but lightly ere he fell
Penthesilea leapt upon the ground,
As swiftly Achilles plucked his weapon back.
Pale grew the Trojans, glad the Greeks exclaimed,
But she stood, deeply breathing, and her mind
Debated if to draw her sword and rush
On death at once; while marvelling to behold
The beauty of the daring on her brow
Achilles called, 'Thou tameless one, be tamed!
Else thou art dead, no god shall save thee now.'
She answered, 'Nay, thou shalt not think such scorn
Of me that am a woman. Men are bold,
All men are bold, and women are all weak,
Thou think'st, yet when a woman's heart is bold,
By so much more it can outmatch a man's
As all her strength is in extremity,
Sped like a shaft that stops but in a wound!
Though but a woman, thou hast cause to fear
And fear me most, because I stand alone.'
She called undaunted, yet her heart despaired;
When quickly came Harmothoe and thrust
A second javelin in her hand; at which
Achilles frowned: 'Bold art thou, overbold;
And surely as high Zeus on Ida sits

And watches now, I swear none braver moves
In this day's battle, nay, alone of all
Worthy my strife. Be wise, venture not more.'
He spoke, reluctant. But without a word
She, moving in his path until she backed
The low sun where he faced it full, upraised
The spear, and cast at him with all her force.
Then taken half at unawares, he swerved.
On the left shoulder, near the neck, above
The great shield's rim it smote and grazed the flesh,
So that the blood sprang: like winged Victory
The Amazon flushed bright, a hundred throats
Broke into one loud cry, and the Greeks clutched
Their swords, as that exulting murmur ran
Trembling and echoing o'er the plain to Troy.

There was such pause as when the ear waits thunder.
Achilles' face was dark, yet lightning-lit;
And all the ruthless eagle in his soul
Called instant for her death; yet she was fair,
Young, and a woman, and surpassing fair;
But she had shamed him: as an eagle beats
Towering against the mastery of a storm
That blows him o'er a tossed lake backward, then
Upon a lull swoops forward, so his wrath
Leapt conquering on a sudden, and the spear
Flamed from his hurling hand; she saw it come,
She raised her shield, but through the shield it crashed
Under the arm, through the tough panther-skin
And plates of iron; in her side it pierced
And bore her down; imperially she fell
Without a cry, sank on lost feet, nor heard
Achilles' dread voice, 'Art thou satisfied,
Penthesilea?' but the heavy shield
Rang on her fallen, the helmet rolled in dust
From her proud head, and the long, loosened hair
Tossed one tress richly over throat and bosom
Shuddering strongly up from where the blood
Welled dark about the spear forced deep within;
And sudden as a torch plunged in a pool
Her face lay dead-pale with the eyes quite closed.

Some moments held, still as deep snow is still,
The hearts of either watching throng, for whom
There seemed a glory fallen from the world
Where she lay fallen, stirred not: spear and shield
Were silent; then among the Danaans woke
A cruel exultation as they saw

The Trojan faces; and one cast a spear
At random; harsh the shouts of battle rose.

But still Achilles stood where he had hurled,
Filled with besieging thoughts that in his brain
Like thunder broke: he heard the cry and clang
Renewing, and faced back upon his Greeks,
Staying them sternly: wrath was in his soul,
Wrath with those spirits despised, and wrath with her
That had provoked him, wrath that his right hand
Abhorred its own act, and deep wrath with heaven
And fate; so darkened inly, like a storm
He came, and standing o'er the fallen queen
Gazed on the shape his wound had marred, a shape
Where strength had into beauty thewed and strung
Thighs of swift purpose, deep bosom and loins
Largely imagined, a God's dream; such limbs
As in the forges of desire should mould
Heroes oh never now to be! So pale
She lay, a life that might have with him soared
Abreast, but all its world of hope a cup
Quite spilled, a splendour ravelled and undone
By his own hand who now, so darkly stirred,
Saw her eyes open on him, full and strange.

Imperiously, 'O thou shalt live!' he cried;
Flung his shield off, with a fierce tenderness
Bending beside her to uplift the weight
Of her resigning shoulder on his arm.
But faint she moaned, 'I thirst,' then at his call
One ran to where a stream welled near a bush
Hard by; but quicker ran Harmothoe
And brought her helmet brimming, which the queen
Drank of a little, though the bubbling cold
Of her own mountain springs hardly had eased
The growing anguish of the wound; when now
Among the Greeks murmur and strife arose,
Where loud among the rest Thersites mocked.
'See, lords of Hellas, see this prince you fame
So high beyond us all, and fawn upon
His all-contemptuous pride, shows his true heart.
A fondler of soft women would he be,
A Paris! Kills, and weeps on those he kills.
We should have left him in his proper robes
On Scyros, hollow braggart that he is.
What is this woman she should baulk our fray?
Let kites and dogs stay over her, not we.'

But ere he ceased Achilles sprang on him,
Flaming. 'Thou toad! ' he cried, and in an instant
Seized with both furious hands and lifted him,
Towering and terrible, above his head,
And as a lion flings a snarling hound,
Tossed him afar to fall with gnashing noise
Horribly biting the blood-spattered earth.
'Spit thy slime there, thou shalt not on a thing
Less vile than thine own soul! ' Achilles cried.
And all the rest, half wroth, half shamed before
The domination of his burning eyes,
Fell backward. 'To the trench and to your huts!'
He called again. 'Go, for the night comes on.
You fight to-day no more!' He shouted stern;
And one to another whispered in his fear,
'The Gods have sent a madness on this man.
Stir not his fury.' So they all retired,
And on their side slowly the men of Troy
Drew homeward: but alone Achilles came
Back to the Amazon, propped on the knees
Of sad Harmothoe, and darkling stood
Over her, where she cast her eyes around
And knew the earth and heaven but saw them strange;
Saw the stilled armies and far towers, and light
Upon the great clouds drooping sanguine plumes
On Ida from the zenith over Troy,
Where wept Andromache; brief evening burned
One solemn colour o'er a world at pause:
Last she beheld Achilles: in their eyes
Meeting, the marvel of what might have been
Was with that moment married, as a touch
On thrilling strings wakes from the eternal void
Beauty unending, but the excluded heart
Heaves mutinous in pangs at the dear cost
And pity to be mortal: pangs more keen
Pierced now Achilles gazing, and in smart
He cried, 'Thou smilest!' for her countenance changed,
Eased out of anguish under falling calm,
A lightening and release. Now not on him
Her dying eyes looked, not on him who stood
Meshed in the wrath of his own fiery deeds,
Passionate, yet transfixed, as if the power
Of some Immortal had made vain his might
And helpless his victorious hands; her head
Sank, and her liberated spirit, where
He might not follow, was already flown.

Laurence Binyon – A Short Biography

Robert Laurence Binyon, CH, was born on August 10th, 1869 in Lancaster in Lancashire, England to Quaker parents, Frederick Binyon and Mary Dockray.

He studied at St Paul's School, London before enrolling at Trinity College, Oxford, to read classics.

Binyon's first published work was Persephone in 1890. Whilst only a few pages in length it certainly illustrated the talents that Binyon would develop as a poet even though he continued to advance multiple career opportunities.

Immediately after graduating in 1893, Binyon started work at the British Museum for the Department of Printed Books, writing catalogues for the museum and art monographs for himself. As well as being one of England's best poets he was also renowned for his knowledge of various arts particularly with regard to Japan and Persia.

His first poetry book Lyric Poems was published in 1894.

In 1895 his first art book, Dutch Etchers of the Seventeenth Century, was published and, that same year, Binyon moved into the Museum's Department of Prints and Drawings.

Whilst Binyon became known to a wide audience as a poet his output was not prodigious. In 1898, Porphyrion & Other Poems was published followed by Odes (1901) and The Death of Adam & Other Poems (1904).

That same year, 1904, Binyon married the historian Cicely Margaret Powell. The union was to produce three daughters.

In the early years of the 20th Century Binyon was a regular patron of the Wiener Cafe of London together with fellow artists and intellectuals; Ezra Pound, Sir William Rothenstein, Walter Sickert, Charles Ricketts, Lucien Pissarro and Edmund Dulac.

His poetic work continued despite the demands of the British Museum and his other interests. London Visions was published in 1908 followed by England & Other Poems in 1909.

His work at the British Museum ensured promotions were a frequent occurrence for Binyon. In 1909, he became its Assistant Keeper, and in 1913 he was made the Keeper of the new Sub-Department of Oriental Prints and Drawings.

It was also at this time that he played a crucial role in the formation of Modernism in London by introducing young Imagist poets such as Ezra Pound, Richard Aldington and H.D. (Hilda Doolittle) to East Asian visual art and literature.

Many of Binyon's books produced while at the Museum were influenced by his own sensibilities as a poet, although some are clearly works of plain scholarship, such as his four volume catalogue of all the Museum's English drawings, and his seminal catalogue of Chinese and Japanese prints.

Binyon's poetic reputation before the war, although built on several slim volumes, was such that, on the death of the Poet Laureate Alfred Austin in 1913, Binyon was among the names considered as his likely successor. It was quite a field. Among the other illustrious contenders were Thomas Hardy, John Masefield and Rudyard Kipling; however the post was awarded to Robert Bridges.

Moved and shaken by the onset of the World War I and its military tactics of young men slaughtered to hold or gain a few yards of shell-shocked mud as the British Expeditionary Force began its campaign Binyon wrote his seminal poem For the Fallen, with its Ode of Remembrance (the third and fourth or simply the fourth stanza of the poem). The poem was published by The Times newspaper on September 21st, when public feeling was shaken by the recent Battle of Marne. It became an instant classic, turning moments of great loss into a National and human tribute.

Today, For the Fallen, is often recited at Remembrance Sunday services as well as being an integral part of Anzac Day services in Australia and New Zealand and of November 11th Remembrance Day services in Canada. The "Ode of Remembrance" is now acknowledged as a tribute to all casualties of war, irrespective of nation.

In 1915, despite being too old to enlist, Binyon volunteered at a British hospital for French soldiers, the Hôpital Temporaire d'Arc-en-Barrois, Haute-Marne, France, working for a short time as a hospital orderly.

He returned there in the summer of 1916 and took care of soldiers taken in from the Verdun battlefield. He wrote about his experiences in For Dauntless France (1918) and his poems, "Fetching the Wounded" and "The Distant Guns", were inspired by his hospital service.

After the war, he returned to the British Museum and wrote numerous books on art; especially on William Blake, Persian and Japanese art. His work on ancient Japanese and Chinese cultures offered inspiration that inspired many, among them the poets Ezra Pound and W. B. Yeats. His work on Blake and his followers kept alive the then nearly-forgotten memory of the work of Samuel Palmer. Binyon's spectrum of interests continued the traditional interest of British visionary Romanticism in the rich strangeness of Mediterranean and Oriental cultures.

In 1931, his two volume Collected Poems appeared and by 1932, Binyon was promoted to the post of Keeper of the Prints and Drawings Department. The following year, 1933, he retired from the British Museum. He went to live in the country at Westridge Green, near Streatley but continued writing poetry.

In 1933–1934, Binyon was appointed Norton Professor of Poetry at Harvard University. He delivered a series of lectures on The Spirit of Man in Asian Art, which were published in 1935.

Binyon continued his academic work: in May, 1939 he gave the prestigious Romanes Lecture in Oxford on Art and Freedom, and in 1940 he was appointed the Byron Professor of English Literature at the University of Athens. He worked there until forced to leave by the German invasion of Greece in April, 1941.

Binyon had been friends with Ezra Pound for a long time, and in the 1930s the two became especially close; Pound affectionately called him "BinBin", and he assisted Binyon with his translation of Dante.

Between 1933 and 1943, Binyon published his acclaimed translation of Dante's Divine Comedy in an English version of terza rima, made with some editorial assistance by Ezra Pound. It was acknowledged for many decades as *the* popular translation for Dante readers.

During the horrors of the Second World War Binyon wrote a poem that many claim as to be a masterpiece 'The Burning of the Leaves', puts in print his lines on the London Blitz.

At his death Binyon was working on a major three-part Arthurian trilogy, the first part of which was published after his death as The Madness of Merlin (1947).

Robert Laurence Binyon died in Dunedin Nursing Home, Bath Road, Reading, on March 10th, 1943 after undergoing an operation. A funeral service was held at Trinity College Chapel, Oxford, on March 13th, 1943.

Binyon's ashes were scattered at St. Mary's Church, Aldworth.

On November 11th, 1985, Binyon was among sixteen poets of the Great War commemorated on a slate stone unveiled in Westminster Abbey's Poets' Corner. The inscription on the stone quotes a fellow Great War poet, Wilfred Owen. It reads: "My subject is War, and the pity of War. The Poetry is in the pity."

Laurence Binyon – A Concise Bibliography

Poems and Verse
Persephone (1890)
Lyric Poems (1894)
The Praise of Life (1896)
Porphyrion & Other Poems (1898)
Odes (1901)
Death of Adam & Other Poems (1904)
Penthesilea (1905)
London Visions (1908)
England & Other Poems (1909)
Auguries (1913)
For The Fallen (The Times, September 21st, 1914)
The Winnowing Fan (1914)
The Anvil (1916)
The Cause (1917)
The New World: Poems (1918)
The Secret: Sixty Poems (1920)
The Idols (1928)
Collected Poems Vol I: London Visions, Narrative Poems, Translations (1931)
Collected Poems Vol II: Lyrical Poems (1931)
The North Star & Other Poems (1941)
The Burning of the Leaves & Other Poems (1944)
The Madness of Merlin (1947)

Poems Set to Music

In 1915 Cyril Rootham set "For the Fallen" for chorus and orchestra, first performed in 1919 by the Cambridge University Musical Society conducted by the composer.

Edward Elgar set to music "The Fourth of August", "To Women", and "For the Fallen", as The Spirit of England, Op. 80, for tenor or soprano solo, chorus and orchestra (1917).

English Arts and Myth

Dutch Etchers of the Seventeenth Century (1895), Binyon's first book on painting
John Crone and John Sell Cotman (1897)
William Blake: Being all his Woodcuts Photographically Reproduced in Facsimile (1902)
English Poetry in its relation to painting and the other arts (1918)
Drawings and Engravings of William Blake (1922)
Arthur: A Tragedy (1923)
The Followers of William Blake (1925)
The Engraved Designs of William Blake (1926)
Landscape in English Art and Poetry (1931)
English Watercolours (1933)
Gerard Hopkins and his influence (1939)
Art and freedom. (The Romanes lecture, delivered 25 May 1939). Oxford: The Clarendon press, (1939)

Japanese and Persian Arts

Painting in the Far East (1908)
Japanese Art (1909)
Flight of the Dragon (1911)
The Court Painters of the Grand Moguls (1921)
Japanese Colour Prints (1923)
The Poems of Nizami (1928) (Translation)
Persian Miniature Painting (1933)
The Spirit of Man in Asian Art (1936)
Autobiography[edit]
For Dauntless France (1918) (War memoir)

Biography

Botticelli (1913)
Akbar (1932)

Stage Plays

Brief Candles A verse-drama about the decision of Richard III to dispatch his two nephews
Paris and Œnone. A Tragedy in One Act (1906)
Godstow Nunnery: Play
Boadicea; A Play in eight Scenes
Attila: A Tragedy in Four Acts (1907)

Ayuli: A Play in three Acts and an Epilogue
Sophro the Wise: A Play for Children
(Most of the above were written for John Masefield's theatre).

www.ingramcontent.com/pod-product-compliance
Lightning Source LLC
Chambersburg PA
CBHW060106050426
42448CB00011B/2633